The Sound of Music®

BEGINNERS PIANO BOOK

music by
RICHARD RODGERS

lyrics by
OSCAR HAMMERSTEIN II

arranged by MARK NEVIN

Contents

	page
Climb Ev'ry Mountain	2
Do-Re-Mi	4
Edelweiss	5
Maria	6
My Favorite Things	8
Sixteen Going On Seventeen	10
So Long, Farewell	12
The Sound Of Music	14

WILLIAMSON MUSIC®

A RODGERS AND HAMMERSTEIN COMPANY

Exclusively Distributed By

HAL•LEONARD®
CORPORATION

7777 W. BLUEMOUND RD. P.O. BOX 13819 MILWAUKEE, WI 53213

CLIMB EV'RY MOUNTAIN

Arranged by Mark Nevin

Lyrics by
OSCAR HAMMERSTEIN II

Music by
RICHARD RODGERS

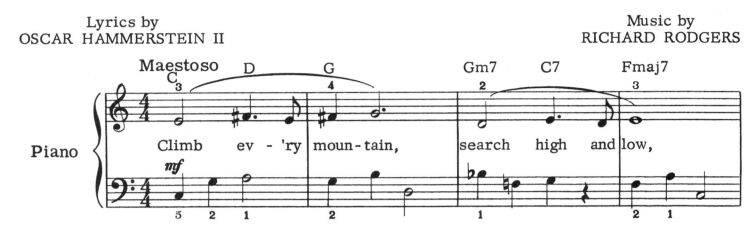

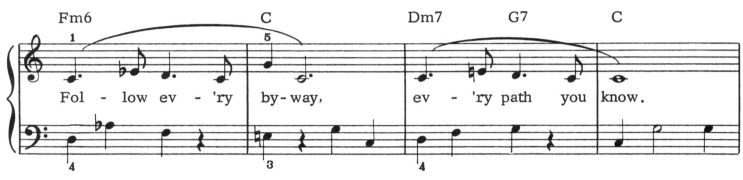

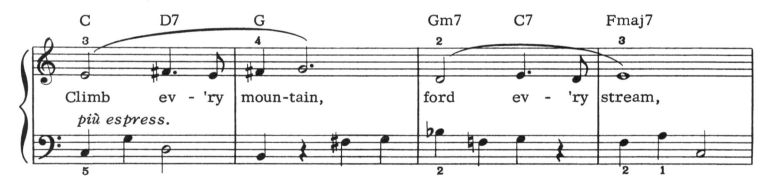

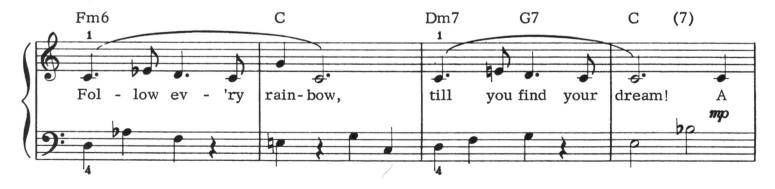

dream that will need · all the love you can give,

ev - 'ry day of your life · for as long as you

live. · Climb ev - 'ry moun - tain,

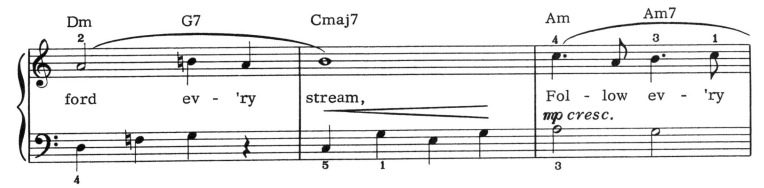

ford ev - 'ry stream, · Fol - low ev - 'ry

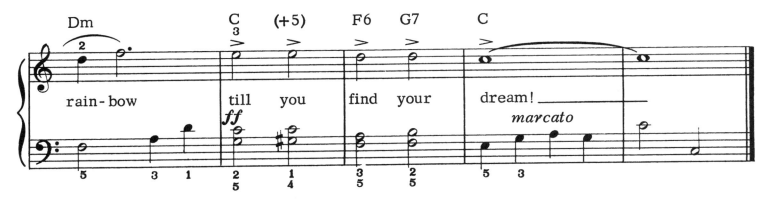

rain - bow · till you · find your · dream!

DO - RE - MI

Arranged by Mark Nevin

Lyrics by
OSCAR HAMMERSTEIN II

Music by
RICHARD RODGERS

Refrain (in spirited tempo)

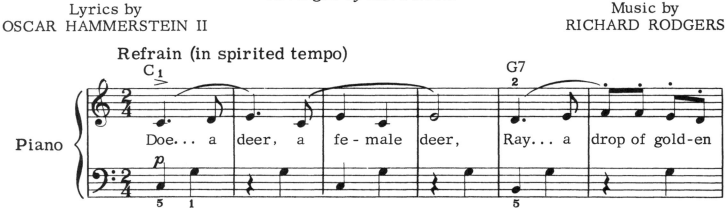

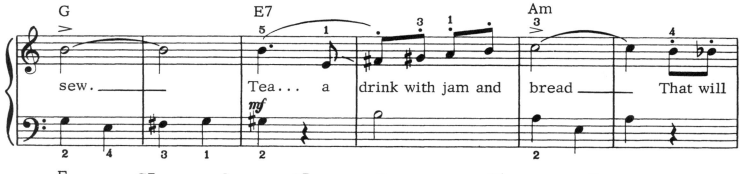

EDELWEISS

Arranged by Mark Nevin

Lyrics by
OSCAR HAMMERSTEIN II

Music by
RICHARD RODGERS

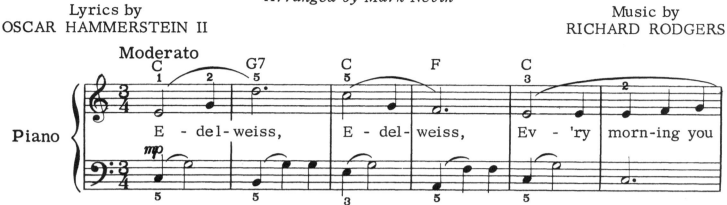

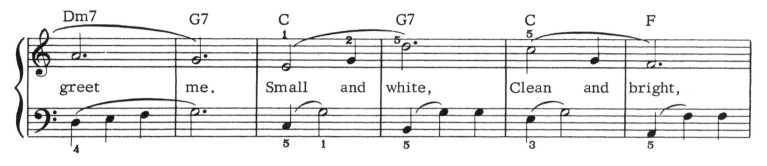

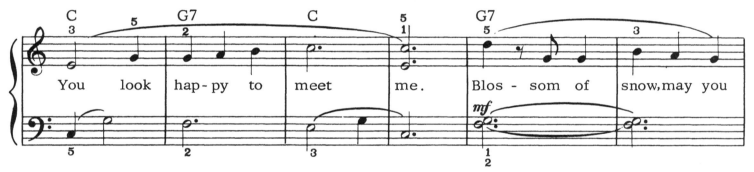

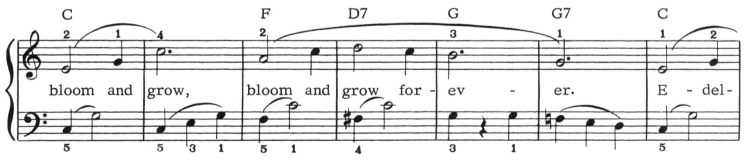

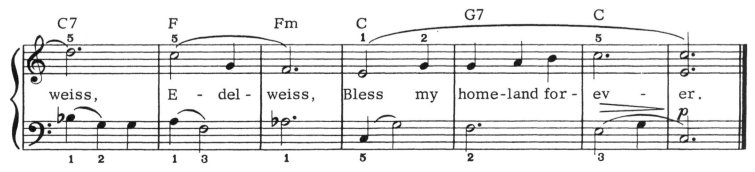

MARIA

Arranged by Mark Nevin

Lyrics by
OSCAR HAMMERSTEIN II

Music by
RICHARD RODGERS

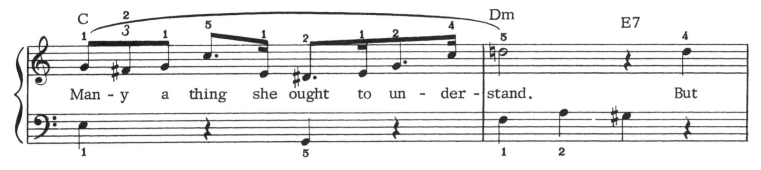

Man - y a thing she ought to un - der - stand. But

how do you make her stay and lis - ten to all you say?

How do you keep a wave up - on the sand? Oh,

how do you solve a prob - lem like Ma - ri - a?

cresc.

How do you hold a moon-beam in your hand?

espressivo

MY FAVORITE THINGS

Arranged by Mark Nevin

Lyrics by
OSCAR HAMMERSTEIN II

Music by
RICHARD RODGERS

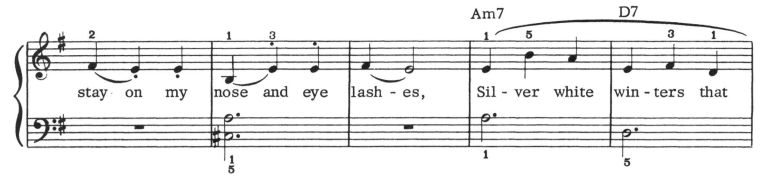

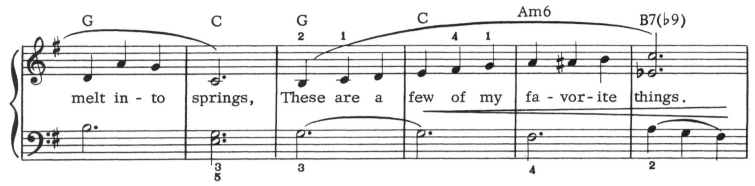

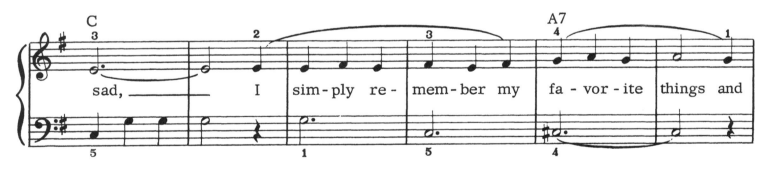

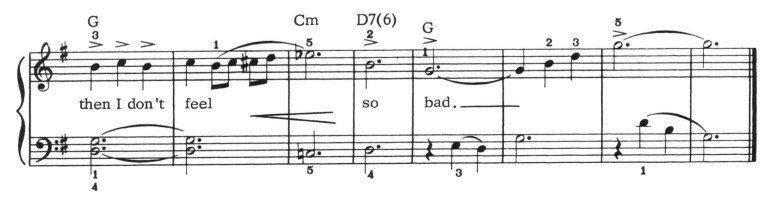

SIXTEEN GOING ON SEVENTEEN

Arranged by Mark Nevin

Lyrics by
OSCAR HAMMERSTEIN II

Music by
RICHARD RODGERS

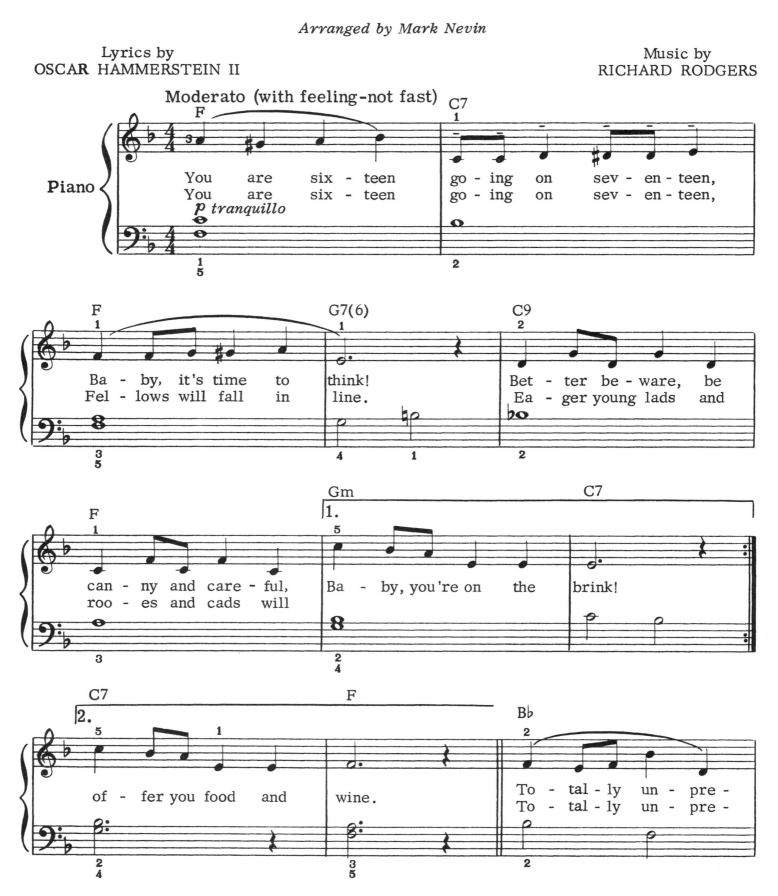

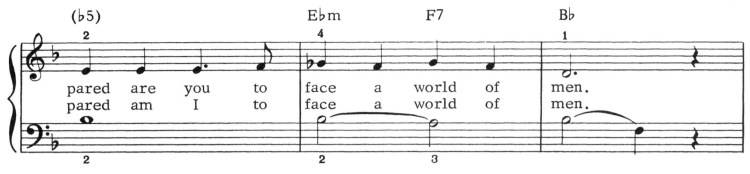

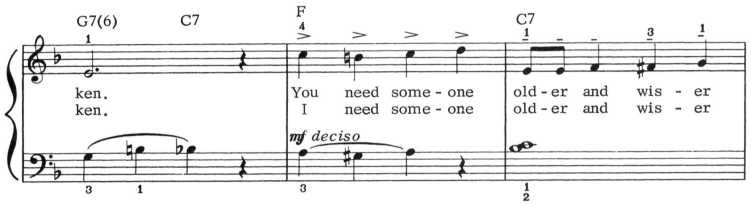

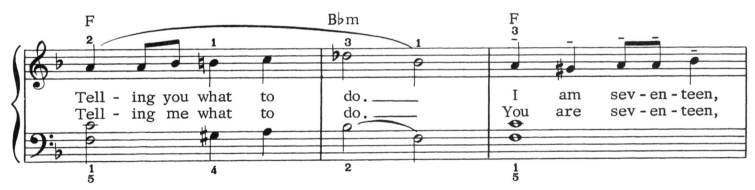

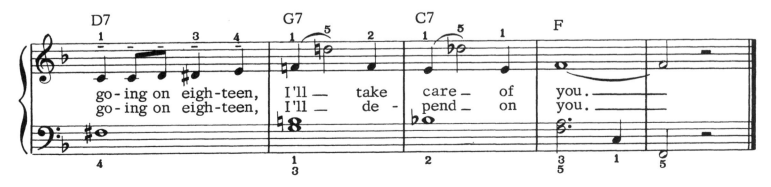

SO LONG, FAREWELL

Arranged by Mark Nevin

Lyrics by
OSCAR HAMMERSTEIN II

Music by
RICHARD RODGERS

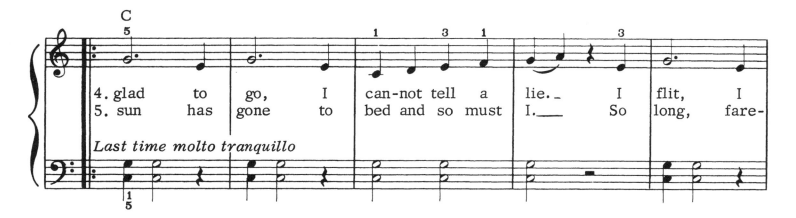

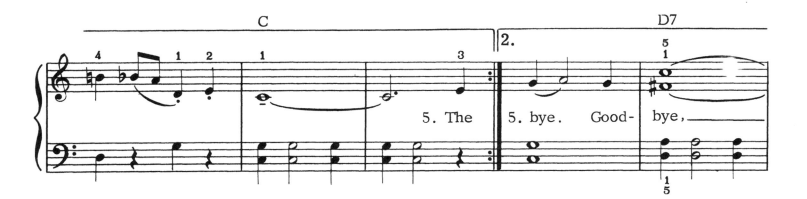

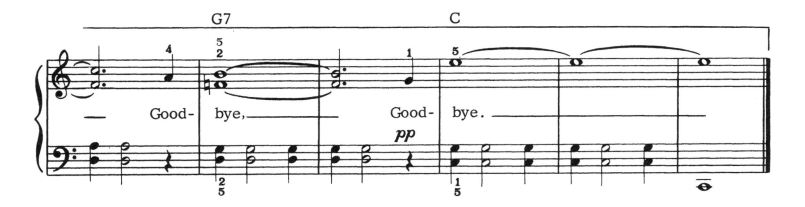

THE SOUND OF MUSIC

Arranged by Mark Nevin

Lyrics by
OSCAR HAMMERSTEIN II

Music by
RICHARD RODGERS

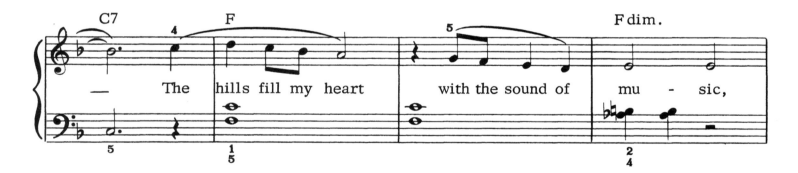

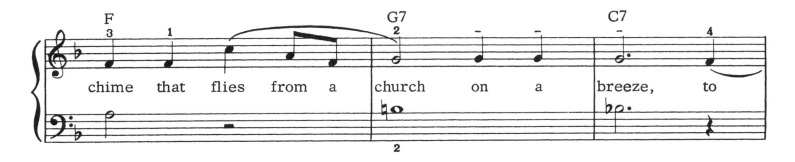

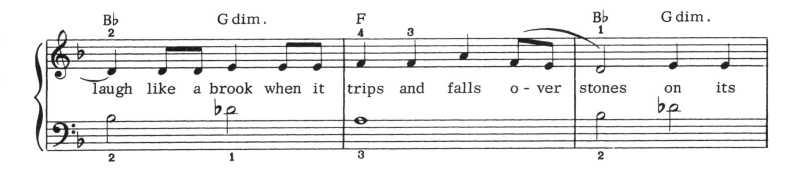

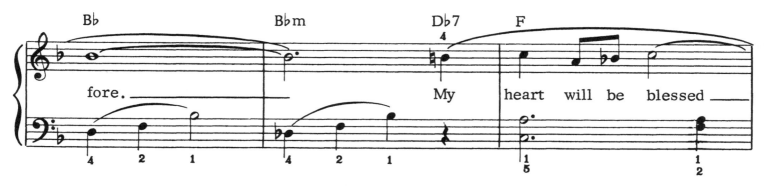

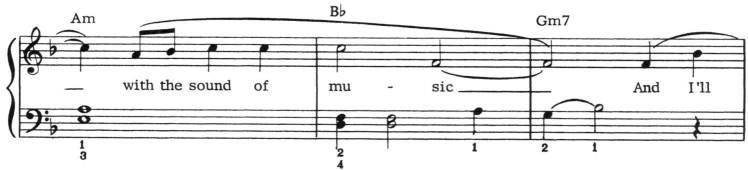